THE

Summer
Solstice

John Awen

GREEN MAGIC

Green Magic
5 Stathe Cottages
Stathe
Somerset, TA7 0JL
England
www.greenmagicpublishing.com

Typeset by K.DESIGN
Winscombe, Somerset

ISBN 9780952767060

GREEN MAGIC

Foreword

As a public Pagan – and more specifically, as a modern-day Druid – the Summer Solstice is a busy time. Not just the events, gatherings and ceremonies that go on at this key time of the year, but also the information that is sought about it.

Every year, television and the newspapers contain pictures of the crowds at Stonehenge, trying to interpret what's going on for the general public. I always find myself trying similarly to explain to journalists in brief soundbites, consolidating tradition, story, energy and simple fact into an easily-understandable couple of minutes on air. What is it all about, why are we doing this, what's so important about this particular day?

It's difficult to put the feeling of the Summer Solstice into words, as is the case with any faith-based ceremony.

The lazy version is to see the revelry and think that's all it is. The truth is so much deeper, older, and certainly not as easy to pin down.

No matter where we stand at this mid-point of the year, our feet touch the earth of our homelands and we feel connection to each other, be they in an ancient stone circle, on a mountain or seashore. Every year is subtly different. Every year, we've moved forward in our lives, gaining a little less time but a little more wisdom. For some, it will be the first time they've taken part in these rites, becoming part of the story, feeling the sizzle of the magic that is passed on. For others, memories well up of Solstices past, friendships renewed and lost, as our planet continues to turn.

I stand on my hilltop with my little family at about 4am, watching the brilliant light in the sky, the colours of the clouds glowing and brightening. Even if there is rain, the greys go from stormy to vivid, paling in anticipation. I can almost feel the planet move forward, as I stretch, hardly daring to blink.

In that moment of sunrise, I feel the heartbeat of my ancestors, the faint worry in the back of our animal brain. What if it doesn't happen? What if the sun *doesn't* rise today? My breath catches in my throat, the seconds seem to stretch forever… and the clouds part as our beautiful star finally makes its entrance. The day begins, the year turns – time moves once again.

Can this be explained simply to those who don't experience it? Not really, no. But we do our best, those of us standing out there at dawn and dust, apparently just staring up at the sky.

We honour our ancestors, our stories, our homes and families. The Solstice cannot be marked with lip-service, because of how very present it is. We feel part of time and space, of the stories of our humanity.

John Awen has put together here a book which attempts to explain this, to both experienced Pagan and Muggle (non-magical person, with thanks to JK Rowling!) alike. The reason behind the ceremony plus the history, fictions and facts.

It can be easy to go through the motions in any spiritual path. But here John asks *why* we do this, looking into the reasons both religious and secular, scientific and faith-full. He explores the lore, the assumptions and the truths, helping us to understand and to explain in turn, as we are asked those familiar questions.

Do we need to be at Stonehenge? No, we can be anywhere, so long as we can see sky. Do we need to be Pagan? Not really – just a human being, sincerely opening themselves to what's going on. And that most common of journalistic questions: do we *have* to be naked?

One thing is certain. The planet will continue to turn. The words here will be remembered, as they reflect the heart of this most powerful of days.

To those who stand witness in body, and to those in spirit, I welcome you. I hope that the words held within these pages add to the Solstice story.

Cat Treadwell
Druid Priest and Author

Acknowledgements

As with creating anything, basically out of nothing, we receive inspiration and an assortment of ideas from a wide array of sources. Writing this book has been no different. There have been several times when I have wondered what on earth I was doing and have questioned the very direction in which this book seemed to be heading, or at least forming.

As the hours, days and weeks went past, even though I was writing more and more, it seemed at times, almost a hopeless cause. Then almost out of nowhere, it becomes the finished article and total exhaustion, elation, pride and many other emotions and senses wash over you. Anybody who has an artistic flair and creates will know just what I mean. The end result is amazing though and feelings of joy take over, it truly is incredible.

As always, the variety of sources gifting me inspiration to write this have been extensively wide and some even bizarre, but that's all part of the journey.

I would like firstly to thank Pete, my publisher and friend at Green Magic Publishing. Without his belief in my writing and walking me through every step of the journey, even though I was left to my own devices, there would be no book, so cheers Pete, thank you.

To all my close friends who have seen me so single minded and so focused that I was living and breathing the Summer Solstice, basically behaving like a man who was away with the fairies, I thank you all as well.

All the ancestors who stand beside me and are with me in all I do, I salute you all and honour you every day. The natural world, plants growing in my garden, the birds feeding and fledging their young and, all the elements that we draw strength from each day and inspire us constantly. A huge thank you to my best friend and constant companion, Pagan, my 7 stone black Labrador who always lays at my feet while I am writing. He gives me more inspiration and love than I could ever possibly give him. Such a beautiful soul and I am so blessed to have him in my life and accompanying me on this journey.

A massive thankyou to fellow author, Druid and personal friend Cat Treadwell. Cat kindly agreed to write the foreword for this book and I am extremely honoured that she did. A bizarre moment asking her to do this for me really as I was reading Cat's books and articles several years before I became an author, and now I am asking her to read my unread manuscript and write the foreword for my creation, it just goes to show what an incredible and very magical life we lead, doesn't it ?

Many thanks to you all and I wish you all a life full of positivity, love and all the great gifts you can imagine.

Introduction

The Summer Solstice, a very magical, sacred and extremely powerful time, now I wonder what appetising treats and thoughts this conjures up for you all?

The very peak and highlight of the year, a time of lazy days, sunbathing, barbecues, t-shirts, shorts, bikinis, flip flops, ice creams and so much more. This high time, where all around our senses are heightened, we feel at our best, joy, happiness and smiley faces are all around and to be seen everywhere. The world is alive and abundance can be seen, felt and sensed, on all levels, all around us and everywhere we look.

We all know and sense the beauty around at this time. Even as a young child I remember now the feelings of heightened pleasure and joy that was eminent and could easily be sensed and felt, I just couldn't put my finger on it, even though it was in abundance everywhere.

Back then, as a young child, you get swept along with the innocence and total purity that childhood brings, on a huge rollercoaster of emotions. Back then we didn't know, understand, or comprehend what was happening, you just sense that it's all good; you just embrace the emotions and enjoy it all.

As a child, each day seems to last forever, a week is an age and a year is an eternity and almost totally incomprehensible, time is irrelevant and simply does not matter. We live for and in the moment, embrace and savour it all totally. It's a pity that we seem to lose the purity and innocence we have then, but then to be able to remember, fondly, those joyous days is a rich blessing indeed but unfortunately we all have to grow up, don't we?

The Summer Solstice is an incredible time, it's a time of total pleasure and we feel so much freer at this time, than at any other time of the year. Nothing is a task nor even a chore, everywhere and all around there a vast array of natural beauty and abundance. Whatever path, faith, belief, tradition, or religious point of view we stand at, or on, the very peak of Summer is a time of rejoicing, celebrating, enjoying life totally and living in the moment.

It's as if we are all young and innocent children once again and for some of the time we stop caring and we totally grasp and live in that moment and we forget our adult responsibilities, even if just for a while.

We become carefree, our inhibitions become greatly reduced and our whole being picks up on the vibrations that are all around. We sing, we dance, we converse more and our whole selves just join in with the magic that is afoot. Yes, we are all more liberated and indulgent at this time.

As a practicing Pagan, following a Druid/Shamanic path, for me personally this is my most favourite time of the year and like everyone else, my whole being feels more stimulated, sensitised and renewed at this time. I celebrate the ever moving and constant changes of the wheel of the year, but Summer Solstice, for me is the epitome of why we are all here in the first place.

Within the pages of this book, what I am attempting to do is remove all the pomp and ceremony, that is associated with the Summer Solstice, and just include some facts related with this time of year, what it actually means, how it is celebrated and why it is so magical. I am also going to reflect upon what it might have meant to our ancestors. I am going to delve into different deities relating to the

Solstice and look into various sacred sites that have been used to worship at this very special time.

Basically, I am going to strip this apart and get down to the bare bones of why we celebrate the Summer Solstice. I sincerely hope you enjoy my interpretation and beliefs regarding this beautiful, magical and extremely sacred time of year.

Our placement within the Universe at Summer Solstice

We live upon and within the most beautiful world imaginable. The depth of the Universe and the cosmos is infinite, we know that and science, which works alongside magic very closely, is literally only just beginning to scratch at the surface on just how infinite and vast the universe truly is. We as humans, cannot comprehend it. There is advanced life and also superior and massively advanced minds out there, but even they have limitations placed upon them. As metaphysical beings, working closely with and feeling our souls, we may have a chance of journeying much further than has ever been thought, or believed. The truth is, once we do intrinsically tap in and attune deeply with our souls, our very inner selves and whole being, we connect and can journey into these unfathomable depths and totally explore the limitless and vastness of the Universe and all that is contained within it.

Meditation and Shamanic journeying can take us into infinite places and for any of you that have experienced this; you will know just what I am saying. We come from the Universe, we were created there and upon our passing, we will once again return there. We all have every inch of the cosmos, the assortment of galaxies and all the plethora of many different worlds and realms emblazoned upon and in the very blueprint of our lives and etched deep within our very souls and essence. Once we free our minds and accept and work with this, the limits of achievability, understanding and comprehension become limitless, there are no boundaries and everything becomes possible. We only assume we have limitations simply because our physical selves, or bodies, are limited. Once we shift our consciousness to our own hearts and our souls, anything is possible and all things therefore become infinite.

We are mainly governed by the restraints of society; this absurd ideology and constant enforcement that is placed upon us to constantly conform, obey and don't step over the line. We govern ourselves and as long as we pay the bills, are honest, respectful and don't harm others, then I believe we can do as we wish and long to. It is our life path and souls longing to connect, explore and embrace all there is to explore, whether that is in our physical bodies, or our metaphysical self, it should be explored, enjoyed and embraced wholeheartedly.

The above is a vital point to mention, as it explains how we, as individuals can explore the universe and other realms held within the whole and greater universe. We are all linked to everything that has been, is now and will be. Within our earthly bodies, we invariably have limitations, but in our spiritual self, we can explore and visit wherever we wish to go. Through quiet meditations and other forms of relaxation, anything and anywhere is possible and we are slowly now, beginning to accept and recognise this. We just have to believe, have faith and explore everything, upon reaching this, we can understand and truly start to divulge our own and personal placing within the Universe.

Summer Solstice sees the Sun reaching the highest point in the sky above us. A time of great celebration and rejoicing as we honour, and give the utmost respect, to the great bringer of life, warmth, growth, virility and strength.

The Sun, this huge mass and expanse of fire, is by far, the biggest and brightest star in the whole sky. Without this great and intense colossal ball of fire, we would not and could not exist. Massive respect and total adoration has to be shown and given totally at all times, even more so at this magical and sacred time that sees the Sun reaching the highest point of trajectory in our world.

As the Sun reaches it's most Northerly point at Summer Solstice, for a moment and temporarily, it stands still in the skies at noon, before reversing and slowly starting the six month journey south, slowly waning as it goes. Held in a moment of stasis, standing there directly above us, burning, shimmering, smouldering and radiating out beauty, light and heat to all of us within the Northern hemisphere, like a salutation to us all, a swansong before the slow sinking in the skies.

Like a rotational, intricate and intimate dance within the vastness of the Universe, the earth orbits the Sun and as we embrace the Summer Solstice, we are hailing and welcoming the solar return. A full year has passed and now we see the fullness of the Sun's return.

Cavorting with the sun closely the moon, all the stars and galaxies within the very universe, the earth dances closely with the associated life giving and enabling planets which encompass us within our world. I see this in a similar way as we know the DNA helix, swirling, turning constantly, wrapping closely, and intimately, almost fusing together in a slow enraptured formation of life and death. Melodically embracing, recognising and forming together but separately the most beautiful, almost erotic dance of life, culminating in a rapturous harmonisation of planets, stars and galaxies. A unity within an infinite universe and a timeless void. This is our placing and spacing within the universe and it is extremely sacred, magical and timeless.

The sun is stationary, a fixed point so to speak, the very star which we orbit. When we think about the statistics of this intricate dance which takes place and of which we are a part of, it is truly mind blowing and at times, inconceivable, but we all know it, just at times, we may not acknowledge it and often, we take it for granted.

Earth is approximately 93,000,000 miles away from the sun. As we orbit this largest and brightest star in the universe, we are travelling at 18:5 miles a second, or 67,000 miles per hour, give or take a bit. How incredible is this when you actually take the time to comprehend this, truly

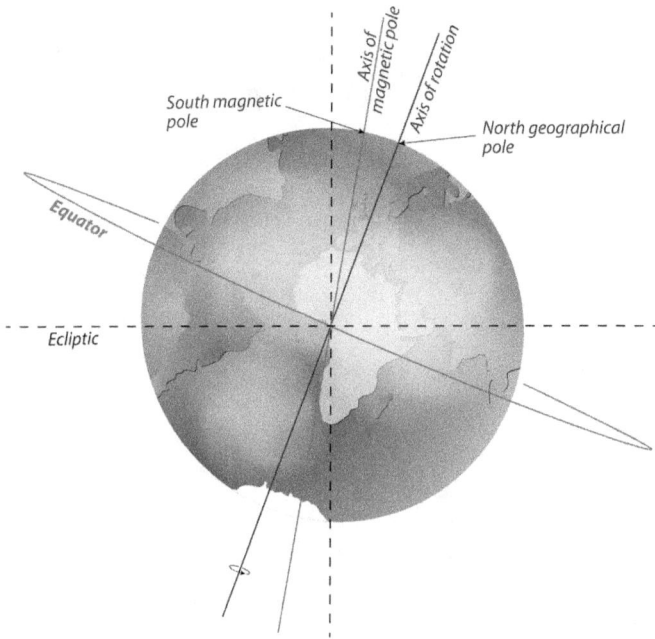

Axial tilt of the earth

amazing and all happening constantly, to us and around us always?

Earth, although spinning constantly, is set on a fixed axis, or tilt. This axis is set at 23:5 degrees. This is in effect an invisible line which goes through the earth and gives us the angle, or setting. Every planet and object has one, like an invisible thread which keeps us from spinning out of control, stabilises and balances us accordingly.

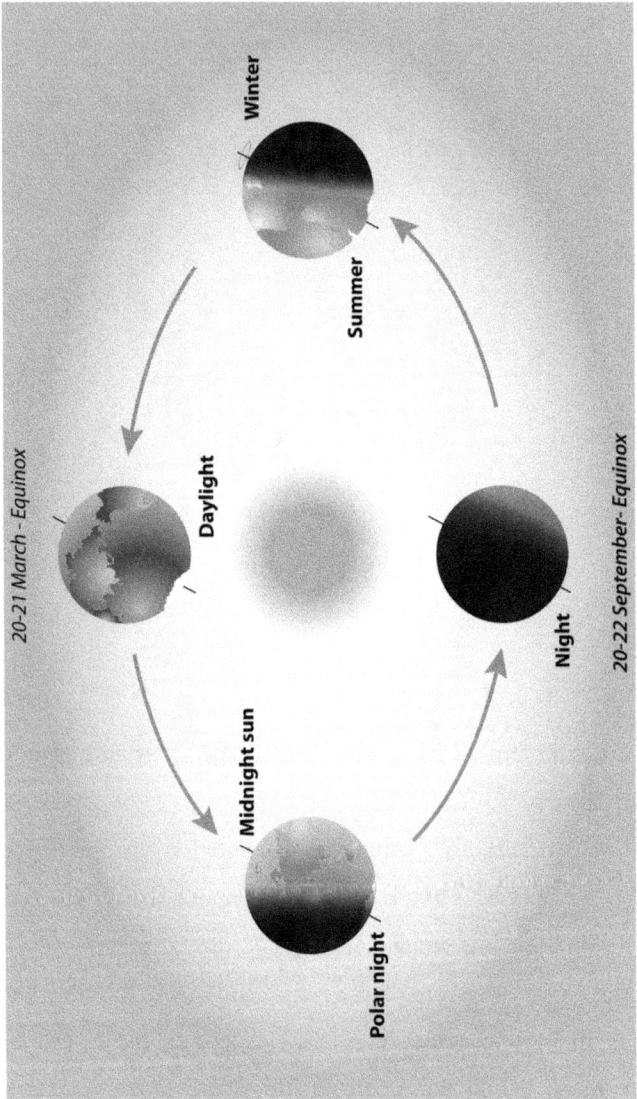

This axis, like a fixed point which basically keeps us in the positioning which we are in and stops us violently crashing out into the galaxy like an out of control pin ball, is what actually ensures that we have our seasons and seasonal changes here on earth.

The axis provides us with the angle which is best for us and is set accordingly to make sure we can gather, collect and harness the best from the sun. If this angle was any less or any more, the days and nights would be a lot different. The cold would be colder, or not exist and the heat we feel would change drastically, maybe even ceasing altogether.

As we spin away quite happily, we remain oblivious to this, but even the slightest shift would have devastating consequences and the way we live and enjoy life now would cease to be. The only constantly fixed points on earth, are the south and north poles. The North Pole is always pointing to the star we know as Polaris, Pole star, or the North Star. This is always a fixed point and from this, we can allocate and recognise other stars and their constellations.

It is this phenomenon and angle which gives us our seasons, our length of days, nights, our cold spells and more importantly, the warmth we feel from which the sun generates upon us. To fully comprehend all of this on such an enormous scale is literally magical, nothing short of. The sun has simply got to be recognised and honoured totally for all that we have on our planet earth, without all the mathematics and statistics involved within all of this, it is nothing short of miraculous.

However much we take for granted in our lives and this world, we shouldn't. Without this complicated, yet easy, passionate helix type dancing that we and the planets contained within close proximity to us sway and move to constantly, we have to be totally in awe and amazed at.

As we prepare to celebrate and rejoice this Summer Solstice, just look at how perfectly set up this incredible universe is and how much we just go along with and accept it all. For anybody who says that magic is not real and does not exist, all they need to do is look around at the natural beauty that is around us constantly and in abundance everywhere. We can all see, sense, touch, feel and taste it. When we open ourselves up to how totally unique our placing is within the universe and the perfect way it is all set up and aligned, then we have to simply bow our heads and acknowledge we are truly blessed indeed.

The Sun's Trajectory

Summer Solstice sees the sun, (which as you will know, is the star around which the Earth is orbiting,) at its highest point, or trajectory, in the sky. This time of the year, at noon, the sun is directly overhead and at its very peak in the sky, it is never higher than it is now.

It is no wonder that life is in abundance and all creatures and humans are noticeably happier now, as the sun slowly rises and takes its time to set, the earth is bathed in just over sixteen and a half hours of sunlight, or daylight. When you compare that to Winter Solstice, when we are literally left in the dark and deprived of sunlight and daylight, leaving us with less than eight hours of the suns light, it is incredible and nothing short of miraculous that this takes place, with most people being totally oblivious to this fact. It's as if someone turns the lights on and off accordingly and the pathway of the sun is missed. Obviously, there are millions of people that follow the sun and moon pathways, so it doesn't go totally unnoticed and it is people like this, who keep alive, worship and hold sacred ceremonies, to honour the natural beauty and trajectory of the sun.

Summer Solstice occurs when the tilt of the earth, or its semi – axis, is most inclined towards the Sun, the star which we orbit. At this time the earth is at its maximum axial tilt towards the sun and that is exactly 23.4 degrees.

This natural phenomenon, or miracle of the Summer Solstice, which is visible to us all to see and feel, happens twice a year, once in the southern hemisphere and once in the northern sector. At this time, the sun reaches its highest position and can be seen and viewed from either pole, the north or south.

Summer Solstice happens between the 20th and the 22nd of June every year, depending on which year we are in and which time zone we find ourselves in.

I am sure you will know already, but just in case, the sun rises in the east and sets in the west. Both equinoxes, spring and autumn, sees the sun rising exactly in the east and setting precisely in the west, it's this that gives us equal days and nights. Now at Summer Solstice, the sun rises north of east and sets north of west. It is this that gives us elongated hours of daylight, over sixteen and a half hours, of sunlight and makes for a very magical time indeed.

Summer Solstice effectively see's us and all of creation around us, at our strongest, our peak and the very pinnacle of all that we are and all that lies around us. The slow emergence of growth that took place in and around the start of the calendrical year and around Imbolc now seems a very long way behind us and almost buried in the past.

If we take a while to look back at our journey up to this point, we can view and see the changes, physically, mentally and spiritually, that have happened to us, others and all of nature and creation around us. From the dimly lit and chilly shorter days of winter, a slow, but incredible transformation has slowly taken place, hour by hour and day by day, leading up to this point, climaxing all around us within a splendorous multitude and plethora of rich growth, beautiful colourations everywhere and strong life that is now fending for itself in the fields and hedgerows and can be seen and heard constantly. From the bleak and almost barren landscape of only six months ago, where all this natural beauty was held within the earth's womb, in a stasis, the first stirrings of snowdrops and daffodil's, it is as if we have merely blinked to reach this immeasurably rich and abundant landscape and time, that we now find ourselves standing at.

As we have now reached the very tip, or precipice of the year, it is absolutely vital that we take the time, not only to look back and reflect upon our journey within each year, but we should take the time to gaze outwardly and inwardly and honour all that has been, all that is now and all that is to come.

Standing upon the highest height and the proverbial summit of the year, it is essential to celebrate, not only this sacred point, that is the Summer Solstice, but to totally acknowledge our own path that has led us to this point. It is also all of creations journey, which are all tightly bound together and interlinked so closely and intrinsically, that it seems such a shame that so many people seem almost oblivious as to what is happening, both in and around them.

To embrace each and every action, to acknowledge each precious footstep we precariously and unknowingly tread, is to show gratitude and thanks, not just for our own selves, but for and to the universe as a whole and all of the Gods/ Goddesses' and various deities that we follow and worship on our chosen paths.

The Summer Solstice sees us at our strongest, our most invigorated and stimulated, as it does for all we view and the wider landscape, both physically and metaphysically. Imagine taking a journey; let's say climbing a vast mountain. It takes six months to climb and reach the very summit and a further six months to slowly climb down and descend to the base. Would you make, or venture out on this incredible journey, without celebrating it, taking notes and thoroughly enjoying this magical experience? I don't think that any of us would step out and endeavour on any miraculous journey, whether it is a physical one, a mental or spiritual journey without honouring what it is we are doing. In effect, to reach this peak, that is the Summer Solstice, we are climbing a mountain and we are descending back down again and we do this each and every year, so it is imperative that we totally enjoy and give ourselves wholly to this incredible, wondrous expedition and adventure.

Not only is it vital, once we reach the peak, to look upon our journey here, but it is also essential to gaze and look forward to the long, slow and at times arduous climb back down. From the top, or summit, we can see clearly and any pitfalls that may be in our way can often be viewed from the very top. From here we can put into place any safeguards that we might see as useful on our journey back down, obviously, not all trials and objects can be seen, but I am sure you get and understand what I am trying to say?

Every day that we awake, we need to look inside ourselves, to give thanks for all that we are, all that we have and all the beautiful and natural abundance that is there to greet and stimulate our every sense and our very essence. We should honour the sacred life we have, make the very most of each opportunity that comes our way and celebrate it all and on all levels. I personally believe that if we don't do this, then before we know and recognise this, we may well find that all our dreams, hopes, goals and aspirations have faded away. We might, if we are lucky enough to, reach an older age and life has merely passed us by and we have only merely existed and been too lost in what really was not important at all. If we should reach this stage and place, we will invariably look back with regret, sadness and hopes that have never and will never come to fruition, simply because we did not live and appreciate what truly matters in this life. Unfortunately, once time has passed, it's gone forever and can never be regained, recaptured or relived.

Each moment, every action, every breath and every single heartbeat that we are blessed to have, we need to be so grateful, recognising the miracle of life and living, to be on this amazing journey is a gift indeed. Honour it totally, give thanks in all that we are and in all that we do and honour all of creation. Enjoy this marvellous journey and in doing so, take the time to recognise each step you are taking and let this resonate outwardly from you.

Midsummer's Eve Celebration

Midsummer or Litha is a very magical time of the year. The great sun god is now at his highest trajectory and we now find the sunlight and daylight has reached its maximum output, which is over sixteen hours which we are engulfed and bathed in.

Litha is celebrated between the 19th and the 25th of June each year. The goddess is now swollen and heavily pregnant with child, abundance is free flowing and is everywhere and all around us, to be seen and sensed, bringing all our senses to life at this highly pleasurable and magical time. The sun god is peaking and is at his height of virility, spreading his warm glowing rays and feeding all there is with his much appreciated light.

More commonly known as the Summer Solstice, this is a huge time of celebrations, feasting, dancing, and singing and is the most popular time of year for Hand Fastings. A very special and sacred time indeed. The days have now lengthened and are at their longest and the long darker days of winter, have faded into the past.

Due to the sun being at his most ferocious now, the lands can be seen dotted with fires of all sizes, where parties and ceremonies are taking place, basically to bring people together, to celebrate and pay homage to the sun god who is adorning us all in his magnificence, bringing us light and warmth.

There are many different names and interpretations of Midsummer/Litha, depending on whereabouts you live and which faith, tradition, or path you choose to follow. It is also known as St John's day, a time where a lot of Christian, or catholic beliefs, celebrate this day in remembrance of John the Baptist.

Observed and recognised throughout the world now, Midsummer is still mainly celebrated by people following Wicca, a Christian, Norse and Celtic path, many more do however celebrate and honour this day, so I have just mentioned a handful of various paths that are the mainstays and ones we will all recognise.

Whether we choose to recognise, honour and celebrate Midsummer, Litha, or the Summer Solstice as I personally prefer to call and know it as, this is a huge time of joyous celebration, feasting, dancing and paying respect and giving honour for all that we have, both in our own personal lives and also the bounty that lies within nature and all of creation. A truly sacred and very magical time indeed.

Since Neolithic times, the Summer Solstice has remained as a very special moment within the cycle of the year, a momentous event, where man has given thanks, blessings and at times, sacrifices to his believed deities for the crops and food, his cattle, health and many other life giving gifts that flow from the lands and his chosen beliefs.

Celebrations and Summer Solstice/Midsummer gatherings are obviously mostly centred in the daylight hours nowadays, but effectively, the celebrations come into effect on the eve of the previous day and have been this way for thousands of years, marking the custom of those beliefs and traditions that follow the lunar calendar.

In countries such as Sweden, Latvia, and Estonia, Midsummer's eve is the definitive highlight of the year and is recognised throughout the lands as such. They celebrate and honour it as their mainstay celebration of the year, comparable only with Walpurgis Night, Christmas Eve and New Year's Eve.

Once Christianity started encroaching into what were then, Pagan areas, the age old traditions, celebrations and rites, started to become obsolete and highly opposed.

In the mid to late part of the 7th Century, Saint Eligius sent out a warning to the people and inhabitants of Flanders in France, that nobody was to celebrate the Pagan festival and ceremony that is Midsummer's Eve. There was to be no dancing around fires, no singing, no feasting and no honouring of this sacred time at all, unless you were doing it in the name of Christianity, which to me shows once again, that there is always someone who is trying to control, exert power and attempting to get others to follow their indoctrinations and opinions.

As with many Pagan festivals, once we see Christianity gaining a stronghold within and upon areas and countries, most of our beliefs, ceremonies and traditions seem to become almost eradicated, or twisted into other beliefs, misinterpreted and often misunderstood. We often see a counterpart ceremony springing up, almost as if to equal the Pagan original, but often opposing it as well. So much of our rich and very festive past and history which we follow, honour and hold in high esteem, is being manipulated, denied and basically lost in translation, which is incredibly sad. It's natural and now is the time that these age old traditions and rites should be rekindled, remembered and rejoiced in once more. We are seeing a resurgence now of the old and natural ways and we need to encourage and nurture them so they grow and can be maintained for future generations, just as we have been able and allowed to join in, partake and celebrate these age old and timeless traditions, we need to encourage others to and basically pass on the baton, or mantle to them, to encourage them to stand alone and honour these beautiful, magical and sacred Sabbats and times.

Celebrations

As a practicing Druid and also following a Shamanic path, I often get asked about ceremonies, Sabbats, various rites of passage and how I personally pay homage and honour the universe, the elements, deities and the wheel of the year ceremonies as a whole?

Now I always smile about this question and find that it warms my heart and even though I have been treading this path for several years now, it really doesn't seem that long ago, that I was asking the same question myself.

This section I am writing now could easily be included in any book and I feel and sense that it is extremely important to be mentioned now. There are several books, articles and various pieces written, covering the Summer Solstice and the other celebrations that make up the constantly turning wheel of the year and I would happily include this piece in any one of them.

As humans we tend to over complicate everything we do and to me personally, it is such a shame. Academics and academia have their place in society, always have and always will be needed, often to give a greater and more intrinsic understanding of various topics and subjects, we all comprehend and recognise this and hats off to them, thank you.

I don't feel it necessary to over indulge and complicate what is one of the most natural senses that we have and share together, it can be pointless and often only serves to effectively frighten people and potential new comers from joining in what has been stirred deep inside them.

To celebrate, tap your feet, hum, sing loudly, bang a drum because these are all deep rooted basic instincts that for so long have been abandoned and locked away within our essence, being and psyche. The most natural sense we have, is our own heartbeat. This pounding and recognition of life and creation, consciously stirs, awakens and invigorates us and can be sensed and felt throughout all of life and within all of creation. It is the most natural frequency and vibration there is, so let us embrace it whole heartedly, rejoice in its splendour and respond to the inner drive that is felt constantly, inside us and all around us.

If we want and feel the need to celebrate, in whatever way we choose, then we should do so.

Way too often, I get asked about ceremonies and people shying away from them, because they feel they may do it wrong. This is, I suppose, a sign of the structured times we live in and are a part of.

My answer, although my words differ, is always the same. There is no wrong way to celebrate and honour creation, our ancestors and everything else. It does not matter whether you are wearing the most elaborate cloak, if you have just purchased the most expensive athame in the shop, or whether you are standing exactly in the right compass point to call in the elements. You do not need to have your altar laid out specifically with all your sacred pieces pointing to the East, South, West, or North.

All of these things seem so over the top and structured, that they do nothing I can see, apart from scare people away and suggest that they are failing, even before they have looked into and maybe started following the most natural path, belief, or tradition that is known to us.

Obviously, the more we connect with and resonate with anything, then our inner selves, or soul will give to it totally, where we follow it, respect and honour it so much, that it envelops us and becomes a way of life and state of heart. When this happens, then we can, if we wish to, use bits and pieces to heighten and awaken us more, that is fair enough, par for the course and we are all entitled to do this. What I am saying here is, let us not scare people off, by telling them they might do something wrong.

It is within each one of us and we should all allow this to flow freely, not only from ourselves, but from others as well. Recognise, walk with, embrace and live with these sacred and most natural feelings there are. We must not get caught up in all the pomp and ceremony that unfortunately is often the case, but just let it be whatever comes naturally to us and allow it to come to fruition.

The best tool anybody can have however long they have been walking their chosen path is their intent. Basically, you can have all the props in the world and spend as much money on your chosen ceremonial robes, or cloaks as you wish. If your intention is not there, if it is tarnished, ulterior or not honourable then everything will fall flat, before you even begin.

I have attended, taken part and been the celebrant at many ceremonies. I have stood and felt pure magic and had intensely heightened senses at the pure and unadulterated passion being projected in and around the sacred circle. To pay honour, to celebrate and rejoice is the reason we celebrate anything, so as long as the intention is pure and true, that is what really matters. It also does not matter whether you celebrate alone, or whether you join in with others. Once you show your respect to the universe and all creation, the magic happens and your path will be shown to you and then revealed.

There is no needing, unless you want to, take part in anything too elaborate, to start with, just follow your heart and keep it simple. The most important thing is that you enjoy, that you focus, show honour and total respect and then from this, the rest will happen and your intention then becomes a manifestation.

Fire festivals

The Summer Solstice is by far the most powerful day and time of the year for the great Sun God. He is now at his peak and his ferocity can be felt all around. He has reached and attained the height of virility and bathes everything in his glowing fiery might, basking everything in his power and glorious rays and swathes of warmth, heat and pure delight.

The crops are now reaching full growth and are almost at their maturity. The bulbs, seeds and any cuttings that we planted earlier on in the year are almost, if not already, at the most beautiful and are reaching full fruition. To acknowledge and pay honour to the Sun God we often light a fire at the Summer Solstice. Since ancient times people gather together and light fires to worship the Sun to celebrate.

Fire provides us with many different aspects. It keeps us warm, gives us protection, cooks our food, strengthens us and gives us shelter from the elements, along with a varied multitude of other fortuitous delights and comforts. Back in ancient times, fires would have been lit and celebrated around to awaken, stir and evoke magic throughout the communities, to bring people together and basically heighten the Sun's rays, as if to invoke his brutal and tenacious power even more. We still do this now and even though we might not fully comprehend, nor recognise why we are doing this, we have to admit that deep down inside us, we do recognise this fact, often though, we don't acknowledge this.

Years ago, huge balefires would have been lit and, as you know, fire is the most seen and sensed element there is. In ancient times, it would have been an amazing and totally exhilarating sight and spectacle to behold. Imagine massive balefires burning so brightly, intensely and magnificently. Many of them would have been visible simply because there were not all the houses and obstructions back then. The air was less polluted and it would have appeared as if everywhere you looked, there was huge fires, as if all the lands were ablaze, which basically, they were.

As we imagine and try to transport ourselves back into those ancient times, we can look and fully comprehend exactly what the Summer Solstice and fire would have meant and signified to our ancestors. Living, working and slowly trudging through the darker, wetter and dreary months of winter, having to think and slog hard for everything you had and hoped for, not just for yourself, but your family and the community as a whole. At times life would have seen and basically been a constant grind and uphill struggle. To arrive at the pinnacle of the year, the Summer Solstice would have been incredible and totally magical. It's no wonder that they celebrated and recognised it as such an intensely magical time of abundance, heightened senses, stimulations and a plethora of many other blessings.

A point would have been reached, ascertained, understood and worked with. So many pressures would have been lifted from our ancestor's shoulders and a routine of work, rest and play would have been achieved. Summer Solstice would have been an incredible time for them; they would now be seeing the fruits of their hard and arduous labour slowly coming to fruition. The cattle and other livestock would have bred by now and the crops that had been planted earlier in the year, would now be ripening and standing strong within the fields. Slowly and steadily, the intense work and struggle they had endured would now be visible and the abundance would be clear to see.

Once the Sun reached the high point of Summer Solstice, everyone around would have rejoiced and celebrated as a community and the focal point would have been to give thanks and pay homage to the great ball of fire in the sky that had granted life for everyone and everything. To have reached this point for our ancestors would have been truly momentous and a massive time of celebrating would have ensued.

Hearken back to a time of basic instincts, having to work hard, physically, mentally and spiritually for everything you had and were given. It makes it easier for us now, once we place ourselves in that position, to see how vital and essential it was for everything you held dear and had worked hard for, to come to fruition and actually see that you were going to survive another year. It certainly makes you think, doesn't it? We can also call into question as well, is the life we have now better because of technology, fast food, supermarket chains and the rat race? I am not so sure, but that's up to you to decide.

There is no doubt at all, that in ancient times, all the elements, along with the Lunar and Solar cycles would have been followed, honoured, acknowledged and totally celebrated. Natural magic was all around and everywhere and our ancestors would have been a lot more connected and attuned with this.

Try once more to forget all you know and all the trappings of modern living that you have gathered around you. Strip yourself back to a time when all you could focus on, was providing and gathering the next meal for your family, as well as keeping a fire going all day and night to provide warmth, a way to cook and also to protect those you love and also a way to signal to others. If you can place yourself within this mindset, we can actually grasp and realise how much we take for granted and how hard their lives would have been, up against it constantly and from all angles.

An appreciation and total respect for the natural world around would have been paramount and you would have lived and worked with that totally and on all levels of consciousness and unconsciousness. There is no way that you would, or could, have taken anything for granted, simply because you would be aware and know that without warmth and kindness granted from greater beings, or deities, you could see nothing or everything. A respect would have been installed upon you from birth and you would honour, give thanks and make sacrifices to the deities you followed, or worshipped and most of all the great Sun God high up in the sky. It was him, beyond all else, that ensured whether you literally lived, or died. His path throughout the wheel of the year was followed and celebrated way beyond anything else. He is the giver and taker of life and we would have lived by his grace every day and in all we done. We awoke and rose at his first stirrings and we would have lain down in bed at night once he retreated, to slumber.

Fire would have had a multitude of uses, as we know and I have mentioned several of these earlier on. As well as protecting us from unwanted attacks from wild animals back in ancient times, we would also have used its essential powers as a way to purify and sanctify our homes, ourselves and obviously our food and water. At times of mass celebrations, especially at Summer Solstice, we would have used the fires energy to cleanse and purify our cattle and livestock. Great fires would be burning and very prominent at this time and we would have led our cattle around a burning ceremonial fire, to purify and bless them as well as asking for strength, virility and safety for them. In a sense, many of us do something similar to this now when we smudge our homes, or burn incense. We do this to cleanse, alleviate and banish bad and negative energies and to restore calmness, peace, tranquillity and clarity to our homes and working environments, it's no different, it would have just been done and performed on a larger scale, the meaning and intention of why, stays the same.

Fire, which we hold sacred and is the representation that we have of the great Sun God always has been, and is still used now, to honour and show respect, along with a way of celebrating a widely diverse multitude of varying rites, passages and ceremonies. Fire walking, fire breathing,fire juggling and a whole load of other pastimes, merely reflect times gone by and shows us just how immensely powerful and significant this element is.

When we take the time to ponder on all of this and really gaze into just what the Sun does for us all and what it has meant and signified to mankind since time first began, we can slowly start to see, sense and feel why we celebrate the Summer Solstice as and the way we do, along with what a pure and immensely powerful time it would have been for our ancestors.

Fire energises, brings warmth, light, virility, cleanses, brings clarity, meeting points, cooks our food and grants us protection. It is no wonder that the Summer Solstice is held throughout the world as the epitome and highlight of the year. We are simply giving and paying thanks to the Sun God high up in the sky for his might, his splendour and strength, light and for the abundant wealth and growth that he so proudly gives and provides us all with every day and constantly. Summer Solstice has always been and will always be his peak and highlight, where he shows us all his might and power in full force. Summer Solstice Blessings to you all.

Summer Solstice Ceremonies

Celebrations to mark, worship, honour and give thanks to the Sun are now underway in the Northern hemisphere, whereas it is Winter Solstice in the Southern hemisphere. There are two Solstices each year, Summer and Winter and it's the Summer Solstice that is worshipped and celebrated more enthusiastically than its Wintry counterpart. Recognition of the Sun God's life giving power and forces, his virility, strength and the abundance that he brings, grants and bestows the lands with each and every year.

Appreciation of this very magical time can be understood from the very word Solstice. This word comes from the Latin words Sol meaning 'sun' and 'sistere' which means to literally come to a stop, or pause. The Summer Solstice sees the Sun God reach his most Northerly point, as viewed from Earth and it's at this very point that his apex does not move South, or North, as it does during other days of the year, but it becomes stationary at the Tropic of Cancer, before turning around and literally reversing to start moving South once again.

Another common misconception that is associated with the Summer Solstice is that the Earth is the closest it gets to the Sun; in fact this is the total opposite, as the Sun is now at its furthest point away from us. When we really look into this and appreciate it all, we can truly see why this date and time of year is recognised so widespread and celebrated like no other time within the constantly moving wheel of the year.

With the most daylight hours upon this day, more so than any other day of the year, you would think that the Summer Solstice would possibly be the hottest day of the year, this is not the case either, and the hottest day usually occurs several weeks later, once the lands and all the oceans have totally warmed up, therefore seeing an abundance and resonation of all the heat combining together and enforcing the warmth contained all around and within all creation.

On the whole, the Sun is seen and visualised as a Male deity, or God. His opposite and counterpart, the Moon is usually portrayed and seen as Female, or Goddess aspect. As with anything there are always different and varying interpretations as there is with anything.

Ancient China viewed the Sun as female and also the Gauls did as well, but on the whole the Sun is seen as Male and the Moon as female, this is my belief and for the purposes of this book, that is how I will refer to them.

From the very earliest and the most ancient of times, Summer Solstice has been celebrated vigorously and constantly. All of the celebrations would have included and been based around the sacred and life giving element of fire, in representation of the great Sun God, whose day this is.

In ancient Gaul, which is now known to us as France and the countries closely neighbouring it, Summer Solstice, or Midsummer was known as the time and feasting period of Epona, the Mare Goddess who represented fertility and is also the protector of horses. This was a huge time of celebration, feasting and honouring life, especially horses and would have also been centred on the base element of fire.

The Celtic tribes of long ago, would have undoubtedly celebrated the Summer Solstice, with a build up of festivities and celebrations a week or two before reaching a huge crescendo of total carefree feasting, drinking, dancing, banging of drums, singing and wild partying to give thanks to the Sun God on what is his proverbial salute and biggest day of the year.

Unfortunately, a lot of these revelries tended to be ignored and almost eradicated once Christianity swept across the lands, because it was seen as betraying the so called, ' One God,' which the Christians were attempting to force feed and instil upon the whole world, basically to get everyone to conform to their beliefs and ways. To avoid being murdered, or massacred on a larger scale, a lot of these festivities went underground and became secretive and it is only during recent times that we are seeing a comeback of these ancient rites, beliefs and traditions on a more widespread scale.

To flex their proverbial muscles and power, Christians announced that this time of the year, which had been celebrated since time began, was to be known as St John's day, in reference to John the Baptist. The date they placed on this event, once again basically overlying what was a sacred time and fully recognised ceremony already, was June 24th. This is just another way to try to remove and eradicate the Pagan Gods and their natural and nature based ways and beliefs. Fortunately, society and people are now starting to wake up and realise the corruptness and forced indoctrinations of this cult and false belief structure.

In Northern America the Native American tribes held rituals and ceremonies to honour the Sun God and these would have been incredible events. With total respect, as with anything these intuitive and extremely perceptive people did, it would have been incredible and a total homage to the Sun God, who they knew was the giver and sustainer of life, on all levels. Extremely elaborate costumes would have been made in the times leading up to the Summer Solstice, with every stitch of a garment being blessed and given thanks for. The Sioux tribe were renowned across all other tribes for their dancing at this particular time of year and they also repositioned their tepees in a circle to represent the cosmos. Once again, fire was at the centre of these celebrations as it always has been. Such is the adoration and respect for the Sun as he truly is worshipped, respected and known for his life giving across the world.

Modern day celebrations have now, along with fire providing the central and focal point, started using what is a traditional addition of the May pole. This pole is used to dance around and is usually adorned and decorated with coloured ribbons, flowers and other beautiful decorations. Again, a pole is seen and recognised as a symbol of the Male and represents virility and strength, which is perfect and very fitting to have a phallic central point alongside the fire, which again encompasses the Male Sun God whose day this is. The Maypole has been used in European countries, such as Sweden, Finland, Denmark and Norway for millennia and is still seen today as the way to celebrate the Summer Solstice, with joyous dancing and singing around the pole. Homes are decorated with seasonal flowers, branches and other pieces associated with this time of year. Again fire features and is represented with small fires and larger communal bonfires, which serves to draw and pull people together, to keep warm and celebrate this special time of the year.

Neopagan customs are a reflection of age old traditions and beliefs in the natural way of life and in respect of the earth, all life and the universe as a whole. These ways are now making a huge comeback and are enticing more and more people back to looking into what has been denied and hidden from them for far too long. To stand in anticipation, wonder and child like awe, waiting eagerly for the Sun God to appear on any day is pure magic, but then throw in many other like minded people waiting and standing alongside you, it becomes intense, purer and even more of a miraculous spectacle. Reverting back to the old and natural ways is necessary for Mankind's spiritual resurgence and survival. For far too long now, we have stood by and become almost ignorant to what this life is all about, the beauty all around and the unadulterated natural magic that can only truly be sensed and felt once we tap back into how we should be living, worshipping and celebrating. There are many different beliefs and faiths throughout and around the world and that is fine, we all have free will and should be allowed and free to honour whichever God's, or deities we see fit. For me personally, there is only one church and that is outside, embracing, seeing, feeling and sensing the divine, the elements, underneath the Sun, Moon and stars. It is here and amongst nature where we become free, we think differently, we heal and everything becomes much easier to understand.

Our ancestors knew this and lived by these ancient ways every single day of their lives. It is by working alongside and with these ways, that we can see what really matters in life. We think differently, consciously and unconsciously. Our comprehension of the world and all its finer workings are shown to us and we become less stressed, easier and freer. The blinkers of restriction are then lifted and we can then view and sense the world as we are meant to see it. Without malice, without prejudice and as it should be seen. It is now time to honour, respect and understand these old ways of living and being. Embrace the natural beauty and the natural ways of life.

Wherever you live and whatever belief you follow, or are a part of, I wish you all a very joyous and magical Summer Solstice.

The Discovery of Summer Solstice

We can only imagine how these timeless rites and ceremonies, which we celebrate and enjoy widely nowadays, first started. We know that since time began, Man has gazed towards the stars, as we do now, looking for and seeking comfort, solace, clarity and inspiration. The skies have always and remain to this day mysterious and untouchable, our depth of consciousness and rational understanding of it all is way too simplistic for us to conceive the complexities of what is really out there, so we really just have to accept, acknowledge and wonder at the mysterious void that engulfs, encapsulates and envelops us constantly, through the daylight hours, along with the night time periods as well.

What we do know is that the skies and stars above have always been perused, gazed into and their movements recorded by civilisations that are now defunct and obsolete, eroded and lost within the sands of time,

To fully appreciate what it must have been like with the first discoveries of the trajectory of the Sun's movements, along with the lunar phases, we would need a time machine. What we can do is imagine what it would have been like if we journey deep into our very essence to glimpse, albeit briefly, on what momentous occasions the discovery of how all these crucial and life changing times and phases were first recognised. Also we can see the enormous significance that they were to have upon our lives directly and societies throughout the world as a whole.

A proverbial light bulb moment would have ensued, but by the time recognition had happened and sprung to mind, the moment would have passed and they would have had to wait another year to see and check on their calculations, probably to see if it was a one off phenomena. This could possibly be why the ancient calendars were put together and assembled at the Summer Solstice, simply because it became a high point which provided a pinnacle to work from.

This point that is the Summer Solstice, once our ancestors realised that it was a regular occurrence, would have been recorded, most likely, along with the Lunar phases, which back then, formed an essential part of the times and seasons of the year. This would have been noted down, along in time with all the other movements of the Sun God and the Goddess Moon, which basically have provided us with the essence of the calendars we know and use today.

Once they had recognised the height of the year, the Summer Solstice, mapping and drafting out the points and Sabbats during the rest of the year, though not easy to do, would have been more achievable, simply because they would have then had a fixed day, time and date to work from and centre around. As with any subject we choose to work with, once you have a point, any point, it becomes a lot easier to track what is happening around and going on with all aspects associated with that fixed point, or moment in time.

Try to imagine, if you can, after what would have seemed and felt like an eternity gazing at the planets which we orbit and all the other celestial beings and deities above us in the sky, you suddenly appear to be making sense of how we are guided by these seemingly illuminated beings. Surely a swathe of knowing the unknown, comprehending the incomprehensible and explaining the unexplainable would have hit you hard, like a eureka moment. To have been wondering of the complexities and chaotic order of it all, then suddenly, after years, decades even of mapping, charting and plotting it all, it apparently comes together and makes sense, in what would have been a nonsensical world you inhabited and struggled with daily just to survive.

The first frail understandings of just how each year panned out and came into being, are probably some of the most ingenious discoveries and the most life saving ones ever made. Not only at this moment could you plan for the harsher and shorter days of winter and the colder months, but you could also work out when, during the year, to plant your crops and encourage your cattle and livestock to mate. It is from here, that meticulous planning would have been seen as a good idea, to ensure not only your own survival, but that of your families and the whole community in which you lived.

As if by magic, which effectively it is, out of the chaos of days getting darker and shorter, cold and dampness turning to warmth and dryness. Countless times of crops failing and being killed off by the elements, suddenly there seemed to be a rhythm amongst and in all the chaos of the natural world. They knew when to plant crops, when to harvest them and the best times to breed their cattle. Imagine all this and what a hugely momentous landmark to reach and what an occasion to celebrate this would have been?

Back in and during these ancient times of our long gone ancestors, life would and could not have been easy. Everything would have seemingly been out to foil them and the world would have appeared to have been full of opposing forces, which were untameable, harsh and extremely cruel, daunting and threatening towards their very existence and survival.

Once a basic understanding of what we now know as the various seasons within the year appeared, plans could be made and a deeper understanding of it all would have come about. Rather than just existing, if you were lucky you could start actually living, very simply of course, but to have grasped this, after decades of failure, would have meant that you were going to survive and within that survival, a routine could be seen, felt and sensed. Far removed from the comfortable life the majority of us live and lead nowadays, but back then, to have food in your belly at the end of the day and a place to lay your head at night was comfort enough and to them they would have cherished it totally and seen it as an abundant blessing indeed.

Once all the mapping out of the Sun God's movements, along with the Lunar phases had been recorded and noted, a regularity and routine would have been put into place and adhered to, simply to maintain the survival of the whole community. Life would have now reached and attained, most of the time, a leisurely pace and all the jobs that had to be done would have been done at the right time of the day, month and year. A simplistic life in what could be a very harsh and raw environment could now be lived and most of the time, enjoyed. A place for everything and everything in its place, so to speak. Regularity is something that, as humans, we long for and crave. We are creatures of habit and I don't think that it would have been any different for our ancestor's way back when they were first finding their feet and getting established.

Still gazing upwardly to the stars and planets above them in the skies, an immense feeling of pride would have engulfed them. A sense of achievement, knowledge and wisdom would have consumed them and this would have been felt, sensed and honoured by the whole community in which they lived. From the darker and very unstable days of chaos and no structure, they would have realised that they were making a mark, an impact and generally speaking, their survival was now a lot less precarious than it had been. A realisation would have swept over them, that even though they could not harness the elements, they could work with and alongside them and a respect would have inevitably arrived. The wild lands that they lived in and upon, could and would now feed and clothe them and the elements, even though opposing and vicious at times, would nurture, cleanse, warm and shelter whole communities.

Imagine now, the sense of huge achievement and pride that would have been felt, the knowing that after years of hardship and torture of fighting against nature, once you take the time to look, seek and acknowledge it all, rather than trying to kill you off, it is giving you and your families' all that you need to live, live well and in relative comfort.

The elements played a massive part in the daily lives of our ancestors and once they had recognised this, they would have become attuned with them, therefore recognising the harm they could reap upon them and all they held dear, along with all the positives they provided also. The Lunar cycles would have helped them immensely and from these, they would have known when to plant their crops, when to store wood and when to make general provisions for the winter larders and stores.

Once they came to these conclusions and a fairly regular way of life, with a certain routine, there would then have been some free time and what better way to spend it, than having a ceremony? These ancient rites and ceremonies would have been great events, times of dancing, singing, feasting and most of all; they would have been times to honour all there is. The elements would have been worshipped, the Moon would have been honoured totally, but most of all, the great Sun God who provided so much for the community and all around, would have been held in the highest appreciation. These rites would have been a way of taking time off, stepping out of what was a hard life and most of all, celebrating the natural and nature based way of life and living. However hard and impossible it was at times, our ancestors would have had and held regular ceremonies to bring everyone together, to rejoice, make plans for the future and pay homage to the great giver of life, the Sun God.

What we now know and refer to as the Summer Solstice, would have been in those times, the centre point of the year and the very compass point from which other important dates within the year would have been mapped from and accordingly noted. Being the pinnacle of the year, along with being the most easily recognisable, it would seem fitting that maybe, the Summer Solstice was the first Sabbat, or ceremony that early man celebrated and recognised as the integral part of the wheel of the year.

Compare now, how you imagine those first Summer Solstice ceremonies to have been, with how we partake and celebrate it today. Thousands of years apart, but the basic and true meaning is, and has stayed, the same. Throughout wars, battles, massacres, devastations and persecution, the key to these festivities has never waned. That key is the very fact that we have been, are now and will be granted and gifted life giving force and energy from the immense, huge and powerful ball of fire that hangs in the sky. The very planet which we orbit around and gain our life giving sustenance from is the great Sun God. When we look at this event, has it changed much? Apart from nowadays being a lot more elaborate the meaning and basic celebrations have remained the same. Long may these sacred ceremonies and rites within the ever turning and constant wheel of the year continue.

Deities associated with the Summer Solstice

To list all the Gods/Goddesses and many other, countless in fact, deities, associated and linked with the Summer Solstice, would be and is an impossible task. What I will do, is list several of them, which hopefully you will have heard of and can recognise.

Within this word we get Sol, who, in Germanic traditions and faiths, is the Norse sun Goddess, the sister of the moon God. This in itself is an opposite of what many of us relate to nowadays, as we view and see the moon as the feminine and the Sun, as the masculine, or Moon Goddess and Sun God respectively.

Another female version and representation of the Sun God, comes from when the British Isles were invaded by the Romans and seemingly placed under their control and rule. The Romans contrived and mixed together an already worshipped Celtic Sun Goddess, called Sulis, they then combined her with their own deity, Minerva, who was seen and honoured as the Goddess of wisdom. This brings us to the Celtic/Roman Goddess, Sulis Minerva, a combined representation of a Goddess who was seen as the very invocation of the Sun and who watched over the sacred hot springs in the town of Bath, UK.

Another female aspect, or deity, closely linked with the Summer Solstice is Juno, or Juno Luna. Even though she is not seen as a representation of the Sun, she is an important part of the traditions and ceremonies and has been for thousands of years. A Roman Goddess, the daughter of Saturn and the wife of the God Jupiter, she is seen as the Goddess of menstruation and fertility. Summer Solstice is the most popular time of the year for Handfastings and marriages and as the Goddess of menstruation and marriage; she is well known and continues to be celebrated around this time.

An ancient Egyptian Sun God, who was seen as the Sun itself, is the God Aten, or Aton and there are, in several Egyptian temples, carvings and drawings of him. Normally depicted as the golden disk, which represents the Sun, he was and is still seen and worshipped as the giver of life itself, hence he is portrayed and worshipped as the Sun God himself.

The most well known Egyptian Sun God, to most of us anyway, has to be the great God Horus. This Falcon headed deity is known throughout the world, more often than not, because of the drawings, etchings and carvings of him. Horus was seen as one of the most important Gods in Egypt, because the Pharaohs believed and were seen to be the living embodiment of him. Egyptians honoured and revered the God Ra, who was the Sun God, so due to this and being known and having close links to the Pharaohs, Horus soon became one of the major Gods in Egypt and closely connected to the Sun. Seen as the great god and as the rising Sun, therefore closely associated with the afterlife, Horus became the great deity we know of now and he is still worshipped and celebrated in and around Egypt today. The great Sphinx at Giza is seen by many as an aspect of Horus and is visited by people from around the world to this day.

In the Christian belief system, or structure, Jesus is seen and held by many as the Son of God, or the God of the Sun. A plagiarised version of beliefs, which serve to do nothing, from where I am sitting, except to attempt to exert power and control over the masses, simply for their own means and gains. There are many aspects of this system, that are blatantly stolen, or borrowed, from ancient faiths and traditions that existed and were in full swing, long before the enforced arrival of Christianity. The Egyptian Sun God Horus, was by all accounts, born on 25th December, this date, as you will know, has now been given to Jesus' birth date, both of whom are reputedly Sun Gods. There are so many deities and aspects of them all, that it gets extremely hard to distinguish and recognise them all and just what they envisage and mean. Many tales and interpretations are written down and recorded, but throughout time, these have been interfered with and doctored by others, that we can find ourselves scratching our heads in total confusion at times; such is the vast array of Gods and Goddesses.

Another well known aspect, or representation of the Sun is the Greek God Apollo. The son of Zeus, Apollo, amongst other things, is seen and honoured as the God of the Sun, providing light and life. Often portrayed and seen as a clean shaven youth, or younger man he is a perfect representation of strength, masculinity and virility, all personified and brought about by the Sun. Apollo was originally a deity worshipped by the Greeks and was consequently adopted into Roman worship and mythology.

In Irish, or Celtic mythology, Lugh is probably the most known and most popular God there is. His name or part of it, Lu, means flashing light, or in reverse, light flashing, as in times of combat, Lugh would apparently battle against hail stones and bolts of lightning would flash across the skies. This has seen him also known as a storm God and he can often be compared to Loki as another trickster. He is seen as a high king and his name translates to mean the shining one. Better known as being the Sun God and also the God of the harvest, Lugh is more commonly known, in Celtic mythology, as riding his chariot across the skies at the Summer Solstice. The time when the Sun God reaches his peak, might and the height of his strength.

Temples and Sites used to Worship the Summer Solstice

Each year on the 20th, 21st, or 22nd June in the Northern hemisphere an incredible event happens. The Sun reaches its highest point and stands still in the sky at noon, giving us the longest day of the year. The first Solstice of the year, with the second being the Winter Solstice. While the Summer Solstice is happening and being celebrated in the Northern hemisphere, it is the opposite in the Southern hemisphere, with the Winter Solstice being celebrated and honoured at the same time.

When we stand in awe and wonderment and watch, transfixed, amazed and deeply humbled at this natural phenomena and incredulous sight, we are transported back into the far echelons of time and in effect, we are watching this miracle with a plethora and multitude of eyes. Since time first began, Man has stood in amazement and bewilderment as he stares knowingly, but also unknowingly at this beautiful and very serene image that is a sunrise. This sunrise, at Summer Solstice, moves anybody who watches and appreciates the pure, natural and totally unadulterated spectacle that happens once each year. As we ponder and wait with baited breath for the Sun God to appear and start his trajectory to its highest pinnacle, we are standing with all of our ancestors that have ever lived. Such is this sight, that since time began and Man walked the earth, all people, past and present, have longed for this miraculous appearance. Trepidation would have built and still does to this day, for several weeks before, awaiting and eagerly looking forward to this breath holding moment.

Encapsulated, entranced and totally consumed, on all levels, by and with this magnificent culmination of the greatest celestial being there is and the very star round which we orbit. There is nothing quite like it and to feel that total connection to all there is, friends, family, our ancestors, Mother Earth and the universe as a whole, is nothing short of jaw dropping stuff.

What we are actually seeing on this day, or any other day, is not the actual sunrise, but the light refraction from it. This is due to the natural curve of our planet, but don't let that affect the moment, nor detract anything from it, it is still an amazing moment and probably the greatest light show on Earth that we are gifted and truly blessed to see and behold.

To throw another fact into the equation, the sunrise we watch on the Summer Solstice, is not the earliest, that happens a few days before and it's the same for the sunset, which is not the latest on this day, this is also apparent for both phases of the sun at Winter Solstice, not that it matters, I just felt you would like to know.

Gathered together, some solitary, in a vast array of different countries, cultures and societies, from Croatia, Tyrol in Austria, Ontario in Canada, Reykjavik in Iceland, Times Square in New York and a host of other well known and some more obscure and remote places and regions, people gather to gaze and await what is one of, if not the most staggering sight to be seen within the natural world.

The Sun God slowly creeps up, radiating his glow, warmth, light and shimmery resonance upon and across the lands as he waxes fully upon what is his epitome of might, strength and virility, slowly heading up and up in the skies. He is beginning his ascension, on what is his swansong, salute and highest accolade and time of the year where at midday, he pauses, held momentarily in a stasis, before reversing, not that you would know it, he then slowly and precisely starts lowering and sinking himself to his setting point, that is due North of East.

During this time, more so at dawn, but also throughout the day, millions upon millions of eyes will fall into what is, at this time of the year, the greatest lightshow on Earth. People become and are almost hypnotised and mesmerised by this breathtaking extravaganza that sees them literally transfixed and held in a cocoon of wonderment and overwhelming natural beauty. For any of you that have watched this once yearly sensation, you will understand totally and agree with me that it is indeed a sight to behold.

The over whelming sensations, gratitude, pure love and a host of other emotions are and will be felt at this time. A natural energy and magic fills the air and our whole being becomes engulfed within it. Many will weep with joy, our senses become heightened, invigorated and totally stimulated by this brilliant display of might that is honoured, paid homage to and celebrated totally. Now all these senses and emotions are not just felt by people following a certain tradition or faith, but are sensed by everyone that beholds this incredible spectacle. A lot of people and spectators are affected even without knowing it; such is the enthusiasm and sheer enthralment of this sacred day. While others follow their chosen path closely, the joy is captured, passed on and everybody feels and joins in with the day and the feelings that are around and in the air, it becomes and envelops you totally.

Celebrations are a huge factor and extremely important to the Summer Solstice. Gathering together, watching, cheering, singing, dancing, feasting and drinking are just some of the ways we can show our respect to this magical time. Fires will be lit, danced and gathered around, to enjoy, come together and pay absolute homage to the greatest giver of life that there is, the Sun God on his solar peaking and most special day.

Summer Solstice sees people from all walks of life, along with many different cultures, beliefs, traditions and paths coming together and gravitating towards some of the world's most famous and sacred sites. There is a huge influx of beings that want to witness, join in and be part of what has become a huge festival, all across the Northern hemisphere to celebrate this auspicious and pure magical occasion.

Some of these people will arrive at their favoured place several days, or even one or two weeks before, such is the hype, intensity and pull of this age old and very sacred tradition. Strangers meeting and becoming friend's and countless friend's, who may well cross countries and borders on their Summer Solstice journey and pilgrimage, meeting up and reuniting. An abundance of people flocking to celebrate as one, together and with the same goal in mind, to salute, honour and recognise the Sun God as he amazes us with his splendour on this day, his pinnacle, highpoint and victory in the skies above us.

Stonehenge

Wherever you live in the world, I have no doubt at all that you will have heard of, seen pictures of, or you may well have visited what is probably the very epicentre and heart of sun worship anywhere around the globe, or at least the most widely known and most photographed temple and sacred site in the world, the outstanding and monumental place that is Stonehenge?

Situated in the vast and undulating rolling hills within the county of Wiltshire, UK and nestled spectacularly upon the rugged and picturesque scenery that is Salisbury plain, stands the very majestic, evocative, breathtaking and inspirational landmark that is known as Stonehenge.

Anybody who has seen Stonehenge cannot fail to be totally and completely mesmerised by its absolute beauty, resolution and incredible dominance of the surrounding landscape. Like a huge power beacon that enthrals, captivates and conjures up almost lost and forgotten primeval feelings, stirrings and basic senses deep within our very being and core.

A timeless and ageless shrine that commands respect from all that come to view, sense and touch these magnificent stones that stand so proudly in their positioning, like a portal, a gateway and a key almost, to unlock the secrets of our ancestors, along with other realms and worlds.

Shrouded and held in a constant stasis, where times literally stands still, Stonehenge offers solitude amongst the millions who visit, simply because of its majestic power and its comforting fortitude of splendour and magnificence. Time literally stops as you gaze in ecstatic breath holding wonder at this superhuman temple. Its fierceness and longevity knows no bounds and as you slowly approach this phenomenon, you become enveloped within its tender and extremely comforting might and strength.

An unknowing, but also a knowing realisation and resonance sweeps over those who carefully, solemnly and respectfully walk and approach this display of super human achievement and engineering, which still defies our so called high tech depths of full understanding to this day.

Whichever direction you approach Stonehenge from it is literally mind blowing and you become heightened, awakened and alert, on all levels of consciousness and sub consciousness. To approach from the same direction as the Sun rises on Summer Solstice, which is North of East, is pure sensory overload. This would be heading directly towards what is known as the ' Heel Stone ' and would have formed, what is believed to be the main processional route and entrance to this ancient and very sacred monument and temple.

This route, which can be a trudge and isn't fully recognised by English Heritage as a route in, is on land that is part owned by the National Trust and has access, though once again,it is not earmarked as a route but is nothing short of magical and inspirational.

Imagine walking over the same hills and downs on the exact same route, that our ancestors would have walked, worshipped, talked and been very dignified and respectful along? Once you tread this path, you are fully and totally connecting with the ancestors, guardians, energies and pure magic of this nemeton, or sacred space.

Hearkening back to a time long ago, almost 11,000 years roughly, the landscape would have been a lot different from that which we see and know today. The curves and undulating hills would have still been there, but thick woodland would have covered the entire area as it would have been the same throughout the whole of the country.

There is archaeological evidence from around 8,000BC that shows and indicates from the evidence of postholes that this site was in use for a long time before then. If our ancestors way back then wanted to choose a site for anything, then why not this area and high point? A relatively small by our standards, but massive project for them with very few basic hand tools and all manual labour, would have ensued of cutting, felling, chopping and removal of trees. Once this had been done, you have a fairly clear and what becomes a seemingly larger and uncluttered space in which to work from.

The posthole evidence dating back several thousand years, can only bring us to the conclusion that this area was inhabited and obviously respected and thought very highly of, without this belief and partial evidence, our ancestors would not have wasted highly needed physical exertion and energy. Quite what they believed this area was, or could be, is open to interpretation and it still remains a topic of debate now and an area which can only be surmised over.

The truth is, we can never fully know what they intended and what their plans were, but what we do know, is that this area where Stonehenge now sits and resides, was definitely a highly thought of and dominant area and remains that way to this day.

There doesn't seem to be much activity, not with archaeological proof and evidence anyway, that much went on around this site for the best part of around 5,000 years. Man would still have kept it clear to a degree and a community would have lived, farmed and survived, of that, we should have no doubt at all.

Evidence shows that around 3,100BC the buildings we now call Stonehenge started taking shape and slowly forming. From this period, we can comfortably know and sense that what can be considered, in the UK, as possibly the most significant and important temple started to be planned for and building began. The work alone was an incredible task and an incredible feat, both of logistics and assembly. With all the heavy machinery we have at our disposable nowadays, this would still be a great achievement.

The evidence we can see and read about now, strongly points to the conclusion that it is most likely that Stonehenge was constructed, possibly deconstructed and built again, over a 2,000 year period. There is an outlying bank and ditch, or cursor around Stonehenge and this is aged around

3,100BC, so this is the linear point that we have used as a marker, or gauge for the building and construction of this stunning and incomprehensible achievement that we see, visit and worship at today.

Try to imagine the sheer logistics behind and involved with this gargantuan project, that at the time, had not been undertaken, let alone achieved in the UK and I think, is comparable only to the great pyramids of Egypt.

Indications point to the fact that the land in and around Stonehenge had been cleared and cultivated for thousands of years beforehand, so that would have made it a lot easier to mark the area out and start construction. Then you have to think about whom and why they thought of using such colossal sized stones, they obviously wanted this monument to stand out and last for many, many lifetimes?

This miracle undertaken and admirably achieved by our Neolithic ancestors is nothing short of inconceivable. Not only to think, plan and actually start on this immensely staggering project, but to then precision it, so that it lines up with the Sun's coordinates so accurately, not forgetting that it was left and possibly rearranged two, if not three times over a period of around 2,000 years, until it was finally completed.

Stonehenge consists of a large outer ring of stones and also an inner ring, along with a horseshoe shape in the centre. The main supports and upright stones, which form the outer ring, are known as Sarsen stones. Sarsen stones get their name from the local dialect, Wiltshire, and comes from the word, 'Saracen, 'which was the common name then for anything pagan or heathen. These huge supports are sandstone blocks and can be found reasonably near to Salisbury plain, where Stonehenge was erected.

These immensely sized Sarsen stones weigh between 20–30 tons each, so this really was a great undertaking to contemplate and when I said sourced locally, that could mean up to 50 miles away. It is almost impossible for us to perceive these sized stones being hoisted and moved today, let alone up to 5,000 years ago, simply ingenious and incredible.

The top stones, or horizontal ones that form the tops of Stonehenge, are Bluestone, an immensely hard rock, which would not have been sourced locally and in fact, the nearest source for this, is 160 miles away in Wales. Named Preseli Bluestone, from the area Preseli in Wales, these have been hammered and shaped to form the fixings upon the Sandstone Sarsens with mortise and tenon joints. Each one of these lintels weighs between 3 and 5 tons, another amazing show of our ancestors dogged relentless might, strength and ingenuity.

How these massive stones were moved has and always will be unknown, we can speculate and interpret, but we will never know exactly. What we do know is that all of this would have required an audacious and combined effort of hundreds of people, all living and working closely together to build this massive shrine to the Sun God at both the Summer and Winter Solstice. There are celebrations at Stonehenge at both the equinox's, but the wide term belief is that it was built to honour both Solstice's. The full culmination of which is celebrated on this day and will be for many thousands of years to come.

Salisbury Plain would have been a throb of almost constant activity whilst this monument, shrine and temple was slowly being built, in its various stages. A community would have built up and rapidly expanded in and around the nearby area. Farming, crops and livestock would have been needed constantly to supply foodstuffs and clothing for this ancestral self sufficient large village and it would have been a vibrant hub and throng of daily chores. Word would have soon spread and people would have travelled vast distances to come and see this feat of engineering take place and to join in and be a part of.

We look at this sacred site now with total awe and bewilderment, imagine how eye popping it would have been to actually see, or partake in this project, which has become one of the most famous and most visited sites in the world to this day.

There are several different case studies, ideas and various notions about why Stonehenge was constructed in the first place; some are reasonably believable, while other notions are just plain ludicrous and total nonsense.

To stand within this huge structure on either Solstice, for me personally, it is the Summer Solstice, you can feel, sense and almost taste just why this stunning temple to the great Sun God was ever considered and eventually constructed and placed together. I am in no doubt whatsoever and having thought in depth and written about just what the discovery of the Summer Solstice would have meant way back then in the distant past, to our ancestors, I am even more convinced. This Neolithic temple and sacred space was to honour and pay total homage to the giver of life, strength, growth and abundance and to culminate at his height or pinnacle and also at his lower or waning point. The Sun God, whom they saw as the saviour and bringer of light, warmth, virility and growth. He whom always bathed them in his glorious rays and heat. He whom bought their crops to fruition and meant they would survive another winter. A temple had to be built to show respect to this great God and it had to epitomise his fall and rise, both the winter and Summer Solstice respectfully.

Sunrise at Summer Solstice

At around 3.15 am BST, two hours before the actual sunrise the very first stirrings and awakenings of the Sun can be seen, felt and sensed. A new day slowly dawns and beckons, but on this day of the Summer Solstice, a very different ambience and natural magic is afoot. The greatest lightshow in the world is about to unfold, be revealed and be seen, for all to enjoy, savour and celebrate with.

Across the Northern Hemisphere at the start of the third week in June, crowds gather on mass at a vast array of sacred sites. Henges, barrows, mumps and cairns fill up with a wide range of people and also solitary practitioners who stand alone at a sacred site of their own choice and making, gardens, hills, altars, etc. All eyes become transfixed and mesmerised towards and upon a point on the horizon, which is North of East. It is at this point that millions of people will see the enchanting and captivating arrival of the Sun God on this day.

Entranced, enthralled and with breath held, people stare in anticipation and trepidation at the wondrous beauty and splendour that is just about to be unleashed upon and across the lands. A sense of uniqueness and being the very first to see the rays stretching, reaching out and caressing our very being captivates all who gaze upon this magical sight. People attempt to become taller, such is the hypnotic state that any sunrise brings, but more so on this day than any other.

As the glimmering, shimmering and radiant iridescent hues slowly start to emit forth, the pulse rate starts to quicken, the heart beats faster and the hairs on our whole being stand up, almost as if standing to attention. Our breath, amazingly, is still being held as we now feel this miracle and rebirth slowly stirring and coming to life and fruition once more, we are now only moments away.

As if furled spears are slowly being unfurled, almost like a coiled spring waiting to gradually be unleashed and cast upon us and us alone. The very first rays of light and warmth are now there to see and we are basked and bathed in the most gentle and tender glow of illuminating pleasure and the first warming's of the Summer Solstice. We now start to breathe again; our heart rates maintain a high, but pleasurable rate as our bodies reach a crescendo of extraordinary and naturally overloaded senses on all levels. The Sun is now revealing himself to us all.

Standing within a crowd at this time is incredible, as is watching with a few friends and also standing and being alone. It really does not matter where, or how you celebrate this occasion, it is the very fact that you are marking it that counts. To see the Sun rise at this most auspicious time of the wheel of the year is incredible and once seen and sensed, your very essence becomes imbued with pure and unadulterated natural magic. This is then carried deep within our very and inner being and we never forget that moment. It becomes harnessed inside and we look forward to the next Summer Solstice when we can once again feed the fire inside us and wait for the imminent arrival of the Sun God again.

To stand within a crowd, as I personally have done at Stonehenge is a totally inspirational sensation and feeling. Standing there on the very cusp of dawn, waiting eagerly with feelings of joy, love and total anticipation is mind blowing and awe inspiring.

Gathered together at times, with a massive crowd, sometimes in excess of 20,000 people is totally mind numbing and it is almost as if the crowd joins together and becomes one complete and connected organism. Joining together, standing and breathing as one whole unit, everyone is eagerly awaiting the first subtle rays, like ribbons unfurling of the gentleness of the Sun.

The natural light all around changes, slow to start, then seems to quicken, as this mass of collected beings is totally amazed and immersed deep within the cleansing and invigorating throes that are the first freshening and comforting rays from the Sun on Summer Solstice morning.

Cheers can be heard, whistling, drums beat out, shrieking, singing and a vast multitude of other natural and primeval sounds ripple into a crashing crescendo of noise as everyone around becomes encapsulated within the raw emotive state of natural celebration. The Sun God has appeared and is being celebrated widely by the crowds who recognise that this day is his day. As he appears at dawn to begin the slow and gradual climb marking and reaching the height of his designated trajectory, he is paid homage to, respected for the life giving energy he bestows upon us and the entire natural world below him.

Waiting at Stonehenge within a mighty throng and a mass hoard of beings is an amazing experience to have seen and been a part of. I will always remember it fondly. Standing within the great temple with all eyes focused on and towards the Heel stone, which is a Sarsen stone outside of the great monument and is the very point North of East, from which the Sun will slowly emerge from behind as you gaze towards it at Summer Solstice.

Wherever you are and choose to celebrate this sacred time of the year at, the feelings are the same, obviously within a large group of likeminded people, the emotions and feelings are enhanced and heightened, but the basic and inner sense remain the same.

There are a countless number of places where you can choose to head for to join in with large numbers of people and there are also vast numbers of lesser known sites and monuments that are equally as special and sacred. The thing to remember is that living and walking this path, which is nature and earth based and revolves around the natural world, has no stipulations and indoctrinations attached to it. We do not have to join in with large groups and I have paid homage and given thanks with a handful of friends and even stood alone to worship at Summer Solstice, basically, it is however and wherever you are able to that counts.

Celebrating

Celebrating is a very sacred thing, however we do it. Every day is and should be a celebration and for many people it is. The very fact that we awake each morning, for me personally, is a huge celebration, simply because I know that I have been gifted another day and another chance to enjoy each moment and grab every opportunity that arises and comes my way.

For those of us who follow any natural and earth based path, tradition or belief we embrace what is known as the wheel of the year, these are eight extra special days and dates which we embrace and mark accordingly. This allows us to follow the seasonal changes which slowly unravel and show us all the natural and abundant beauty that is there for us all to enjoy. The highlight and most celebrated date, from where I am sitting must be the Summer Solstice.

Summer is here and we all feel positive and our inhibitions are lessened. A time of joyous celebrations where we can sense the purity, naturalness and total fruition that is before our very eyes, and within ourselves and others whole beings. All around us everything is an extremely heightened state and this peaks as the Sun God starts his processional ascent upon this very day.

Climbing to his very peak on the Summer Solstice, he reaches his maturity and within this, everywhere and everyone culminates and reaches a high alongside with him. Like a rapturous applauding, we can totally become immersed and encapsulated with the vibrancy that is in abundance everywhere. A truly magical time, and a very sacred occasion.

To be a part of and partake of this day is just so beautiful. However we choose to mark and celebrate this poignant time of the year and our very lives, is irrelevant, it is the simple fact that we do that really matters the most.

There are huge ceremonies going on and thousands of people will flock together to marvel and watch this phenomenal sight. Smaller groups and solitary celebrations are always good as well and often, I have attended smaller meetings and felt more of a connection and a much deeper feeling and sense of beauty and warmth, simply because everyone there seems to be more attuned and obviously, there are not the distractions which you can and do invariably get with larger numbers.

Nowadays, I tend to celebrate and mark the ever turning wheel of the year with special friends and loved ones. I find that way too many of these sacred ceremonies seem to be turning into nothing more than farcical excuses for getting drunk, exploiting others and also that a lot of egos are getting in the way of allowing others to celebrate from the heart, what is a time to be totally and utterly respectful. Everybody is allowed to join in as they wish and see fit, but to make a mockery of what is natural and sacred goes against everything that I believe in and hold special to me.

I have celebrated with tens of thousands of people and it has been awe inspiring and thoroughly enjoyable. The aftermath later on though is nothing short of a travesty and an insult, both to the site and most of the people who have attended. I have witnessed people climbing upon these ancient monuments, spitting and being sick on and around them. I have seen fights break out, bottles being smashed against sacred stones and sites being violated.

The litter that gets left behind is appalling and should not happen. It makes a total ridicule of the whole thing.

These beautiful, timeless and ageless places and temples are unfortunately, not seen as sacred by many and it becomes nothing more than an excuse to go and have a disrespectful party on sacred land. I can fully see and comprehend why so many sites have varied and restrictive access. It has now sadly, got to this point and is needed simply to protect and stop wilful damage of our very heritage. I will say though, the majority of people who attend and visit anywhere, are courteous, respectful and there for the right reasons. As with anything, or any walk of life, there are and always will be the minority of people who seem so wrapped up in themselves and their own importance and arrogance that nothing else seems to matter and they become oblivious to their actions. Oh for the ignorant in this world.

To live as freely as we do and to be able to follow our chosen path is a huge blessing, which the majority of us living in the modern world today are able to do. There is a magical world around us and we can explore it at will and are able to partake in the countless gifts which it has to offer. To walk within nature and enjoy the delights which are there for us all is a rich blessing indeed and to say Thank you, to stand under the skies, surrounded by the natural world and with the elements close by is the perfect and only way we can give thanks. Our lives are busy, the world is a tough and hard place, so to enjoy, savour and pay homage for all that we have and are, becomes a way of life and a state of heart for countless people.

A ceremony, whether it is to celebrate the Summer Solstice, or any other special time, does not have to be contentious, over elaborated or difficult. It is the intent that matters and so long as you are respectful and you give thanks and show that you are honouring the God/Goddess and chosen deities, along with the world and universe, that is what matters.

As much can be done in your own garden as can be done at any large public ritual or ceremony. It is nice to wear a robe, or cloak and it is enjoyable also to be able to perform and take part in a public ceremony, but please do not think for a minute that it has to be done. Wherever you give thanks and however you acknowledge the sanctity of an occasion, it matters and those that you are honouring see and feel this.

Celebrate often and as you watch the wheel of the year go by, recognise and show respect by giving thanks and paying homage to all the world and natural Earth which holds and cradles you each and every day.

This Summer Solstice, honour and celebrate in whatever way feels right for you to mark the Sun God's journey to his highest peak and join him in celebration as he slowly and assertively ascends high up into the sky. Sense the natural world around you and as he reaches his pinnacle of the year, sense your own journey along with his. Reflect back upon how far you have come since the long and darker days of winter and look forward to what is to come and let the positive thoughts you have slowly manifest, nurturing them and bringing them to fruition in the days, weeks and months ahead.

Coming together

As we wait this Summer Solstice, breath held and heart rate gaining momentum, we are connecting with not only the natural world, but also the multitude and vast array of people around and in the Northern Hemisphere. We are all poised with eager anticipation for those few fleeting moments when the Sun slowly and majestically puts in an appearance and can be seen in the dawn skies.

From the very start of time, when Mankind was totally oblivious to everything that he found happening to and around him, when he felt lost, naïve, vulnerable and totally exposed, this is the same resonation that sweeps over us as the day begins to break. Feelings of being lost can grab us at any time, especially when we feel so small, fragile and insignificant compared to what is going on around us.

Naïve because we expect it to happen, but it still enthrals and captivates us when it does. Vulnerable due to the crowds we may find ourselves in and feelings of exposure as we stand there almost awaiting for a birth.

A heartbeat is present and pounds constantly within all creation as well as our own personal bodies. On a sacred day, this throb and pulsing can be felt more strongly as we stand waiting for magic to totally fill us and the very air that we inhale. A strong resonance and connection with all that has been, is now and will be again fills us utterly and consumes every single cell of our bodies. A glorious exaltation and eagerness grabs us and fills us wholly.

Across the lands and way back through the very mists of time, we stand waiting for this very moment. The same moment that millions of other living beings are waiting for, to watch, gaze and capture the very essence of the sun rise on Summer Solstice. We feel our ancestors more closely at times like these, knowing and sensing they too have eagerly anticipated and stood still and resolute as they watch this very same spectacle unfold. A link and connection so intrinsically deep that we feel it on all our levels, physically and metaphysically.

Whether we stand alone, within a small group, or a large group of thousands, the raw and heightened sense is the same, one of knowing and seeing the unknown and also respecting it, for as it reveals itself, it is known. We remember, recognise and honour the moment totally. A mass connection engulfs and washes over us invoking swathes of heat, love, passion and bewilderment. Long awaited moments like this conjure up natural passions that have lain dormant deep within our very psyche since our souls first gazed upon this natural wonder. The feelings have never left us, they are always with and inside us, and they just get reremembered each time we invoke the passion that rekindles them.

Engulfed once more as we watch the sunrise at Summer Solstice, we are transported back and forth within time. Back to a time we recognise, but are unsure of, simply because in this body vessel, we are not too sure of it and the feelings are not familiar to us. Catapulted forwards in time as we sense all the sun rises to come, yet our physical self still remains in the now. A vast multitude of base emotions send us into a dizzy plethora of over sensitised feelings. Seeing the unseen, recalling the once seen, sensing the feelings long departed and being a part of it all, the then, the now and the what is to come.

It is no wonder we often find ourselves unknowingly struggling to stand up as these powerful emotions and feelings rock us to our very core. Embracing the whole universal language and tuning into all that has ever happened, swamped, yet secure and cleansed in all that is happening to and with us. Stepping almost out of our physical selves, the metaphysical being takes over, leaving us temporarily. This allows us to savour the very moment, before it is gone and passed by.

Captured and installed within us, along with a vast amount of visual delights, we store and register each one of these truly magical sights and the feelings stay with us. Each time we watch a sunrise, or another sacred occasion, we are pulling together a huge amount of memories, which become intensified and magnified each and every time we partake and connect once again.

The natural magic and passions that come to the forefront and are shaken about are there to help us see, and sense, the abundant beauty that is all around us and in all we do. The sun, moon and all the elements are there to inspire and awaken our inner being and connect us with every molecule that is alive now and has gone before us.

The tumultuous reverberation upon our very being at a heightened time of celebration such as the Summer Solstice is nothing short of tremendous, yet also melancholic. The almost violent surges and waves of transformation as we see, acknowledge and accept what is happening in and around us are totally pleasurable, providing us with a huge natural high.

Upon such an event and sacred time, even if we are celebrating alone, we are connecting totally with many varied cultures, faiths, traditions, cultures and people under the same skies. This is all part of the collective network of consciousness that is invisibly covering this whole world, along with other worlds and realms. Like ripples from a stone being tossed into the ocean people we will never know or meet, are picking up and feeling the wave of positivity being created and thrown out into the world.

No matter what anybody believes, or claims to not believe, this earth and natural based way of life and living is simply undeniable. People have and always will look towards the skies, often just for ideas, inspirations and generally seeking solace and comfort.

Since time first began and Mankind first took those tentative first steps, we have always been seeking, longing for and yearning for answers and comfort. This can only be found within nature and the natural world is the only place we can truly find it. Modern society is an incredible place to be living. We have all of the high tech gadgets and tools, which easily enable us to find answers, talk face to face with people in an instant and send messages around the world. It is incredible and to be alive today is so humbling.

On the flip side of all this, we have now removed ourselves further than ever before from the world and what is really important in life. People are so immersed in their phones and I-pads that they have become totally oblivious to anything natural around them. We can at times, all be guilty of this.

We all need to disconnect from all this technology at times and go back to our natural earthen roots. It is while we visit, and spend time, in nature that we truly connect once more. The feelings of total peace, calm, serenity, healing and a vast array of other powerful emotions and senses are awakened while we stand within the trees, alongside rivers and on top of grassy mounds. There is nothing like celebrating under the natural skies, being embraced by all the elements and honouring the universe as a whole, along with all the deities you personally believe in. This is how we are supposed to be giving thanks, paying homage and dedicating ourselves to the earth, our chosen God/Goddess and all of creation as a whole.

We need now, as a whole to start looking back and re – introducing ourselves, our families, loved ones and friends to the old ways and ways of our ancestors. I am not saying throw away and not use the new technology, as I believe it all has a purpose in this day and age. What I am saying, is we need to move away from the constant distractions of TV, social media sites and the rest of technology and make a point of venturing out into the great outdoors. Time to rekindle the senses, awaken, stir and invigorate our whole beings, consciously and subconsciously. Feed our physical and metaphysical selves. This can only be achieved outside under the great canopy of natural skies.

Whether we go into a forest, or even a garden, whatever the size, if we can, that is all it takes. Just to absorb all the natural wonders around. Taste the air, smell and savour the aroma from the grass and flowers. Feel and touch the soil, if possible. What is most important is to just breath and let the air flow in and out of your body and recognise the spirit and very essence that is within us all, but at times can become dormant.

Recently, I took part in what is being hailed as the world's first online festival. It was arranged and overseen by the Pagan Federation and their disabilities team. They set out to bring people together and have the chance to join in and connect with one another. This went viral and was enjoyed by many faiths and beliefs from all over the world. This event was nothing short of ground breaking and it involved live on line talks, one of which I was proud to be asked to give and did so. There were prize giveaways, questions and answers and a live performance from a band. The response to this event was incredible and it achieved its aim by giving disabled people the chance to join in and celebrate together. Unfortunately, there are many, who for no fault of their own, find getting out very difficult, or even impossible. I can see these online festivals/ceremonies really catching on and I sincerely hope that they do. Nobody should be made to feel totally ostracised, no matter how ill and poorly they may be. With all the gadgets we have nowadays, there is no reason at all why they should be.

Conclusion

The Summer Solstice is a very magical, sacred and enlightening time. For me personally it is the very peak of the wheel of the year, which I and millions of others follow and mark at each turn. A great time of reflection, reviewing what has gone and looking forward with heightened energies to what is to come. As the Sun reaches and achieves his pinnacle, we celebrate with him and feel the abundant strength from him and within ourselves.

A truly magical and extremely auspicious occasion and event. As we stand to watch him gaining his maximum height, we are taken on a huge spiritual journey, one that totally connects us to our inner and outer selves and the world as a whole.

I have tried to explain what the first awakenings and realisation of Summer Solstice might have felt like for our ancestors. It is these long gone ancient ones that we now owe so much to. We can now rejoice together and marvel at much of this beautiful world we are blessed to walk upon and inhabit, because they ventured first and noted it.

To remember and celebrate the ancestors is part of what any celebration is about and for, simply because without them, we would and could not exist. Invoke their energy within you, not just at a sacred ceremony, but every day and in all we do.

I have thoroughly enjoyed writing this book and it has taken me on an incredible journey, which is what happens with any genre of creativity which we may find ourselves undertaking.

Wherever you find yourself marking this Summer Solstice and whatever faith, belief, or tradition you happen to follow, I wish you a very magical and sacred Summer Solstice. If you have any questions, or would like to ask me something about this book, please feel free to e-mail me at spiritoftheawen@yahoo.com

Summer Solstice Blessings and much love to you all.

John Awen   / | \

Midsummer Fruit Bread

4 Mugs of strong white flour
500ml of Buttermilk – available from
supermarkets
1 teaspoonful of Bicarbonate of soda
4 dessertspoons of honey
2 handfuls of mixed dried fruit
1 handful of mixed peel
Teaspoon caster sugar
Desert spoonful of chopped nuts
One orange Ribbon
One yellow ribbon

Place sieved flour and bicarbonate of soda and dried fruit in a large bowl and make a well in the centre. Shake buttermilk carton then pour into a jug add the honey and stir well then pour into the centre leaving a little for glazing, mix with your hands until springy.

Turn on to a floured board. Pat with both hands into a round shape. Glaze the top with the remaining mixture and sprinkle with chopped nuts and sugar. Place on a greased baking tray and pop into a moderate oven for about 20–25 minutes.

Keep a watchful eye on it, when ready your bread will change colour and sound hollow when you tap the bottom. When the bread has cooled but still a little warm wrap with greaseproof paper and tie your ribbons across the top in a bow. Best eaten warm it also reheats really well.

www.ingramcontent.com/pod-product-compliance
Lightning Source LLC
La Vergne TN
LVHW021525080426
835509LV00018B/2660